# A.I.M. HIGH

## "Create A Blueprint To Conquer Your Life"

**By**
**Shardae Womack, MPA, JD**

Pastor Julia,

Thank you for your love and support. I appreciate all that you've done over the years to ~~make~~ contribute to the woman of God I am today. I especially thank you for sharing the prophetic word in 2014 about the books I will write. One down, volumes to go! lol. I pray that God return hundred fold every donation you made in my life spiritually, mentally, emotionally and physically. I thank you and bless God for allowing me to know you.

Love, Leaves, Legacy

# A.I.M.

## ACCOUNTABLE IDEAS MANIFEST

A.I.M. High, by Shardae Womack
Published by The Legacy Project

For permissions contact:
Info@shardaewomack.com
ISBN: 978-1-948777-02-5

# DEDICATION

*To my courageous parents, my lovely grandmothers, my invincible siblings, my phenomenal mentors, and my unique sister friends and mentees.*

*Thank You God for including me in your Master vision.*

# TABLE OF CONTENTS

# Dear Visionary,

My prayer for you is that God gives you the faith to speak life and move mountains as you pursue the visions He has given you. I want you to unapologetically, break ground in new territory. As you branch out, may you possess the power, love, and sound mind of God to accomplish every goal, despite the fear that may be present.

When the excitement wears off, and the workload seems unbearable, and the phone calls and emails overflow, may the blessings not feel like burdens and may you find joy in the midst of your to- do list.

Fiercely pursue each chapter of your life and let the destination be the goal but the journey be your reward. When you conquer territory, both near and far, may you always pay homage to those who've paved the way. As you write and speak, may the seeds you've planted fall on fertile soil, and grow into fruit that will one day feed the next generation.

Where your eyes see, may your spirit grasp the vision. Where your ears hear, may your spirit listen. Where your hands touch, may you relate. Where your heart feels, may your spirit connect.

Choose to love anyway, Choose to see the light anyway. Choose to write the truth anyway. Choose to capture the best of the experience. Choose you anyway.

Lord, may strength, laughter, and wisdom be their portion. Thank you for your infinite and divine wisdom that will guide them and order their steps. Thank you for shining light on every dim and dark situation. Thank you for the needed provisions to make all of their hearts desires come true.

I am elated that you are stepping into a new journey to live your new and exceedingly abundant life.

LOVE LEAVES A LEGACY,

**Shardae Womack**

# INTRODUCTION

AIM High was created out of a desire to see the many visions, that God has placed in all of us, manifest as we fulfill our purpose. We often have great ideas and big dreams, but we rarely see them come to fruition. Many times this is because our dreams appear to be impossible. We have settled for where we are instead of aiming higher because of that perception and our subsequent fear. We have allowed fear to intimidate us, discourage us, and push us to abort the mission.

We believe the lies that say "it's too late to start," "the dream is too big," or "you don't have the resources to achieve it." We feed into these dark thoughts and inevitably embody their malice as if it had been sourced from within us. This self-destruction evolves into a complacency that we barely notice—as most people have fallen victim to it.

Unfortunately, we become comfortable living mediocre lives—wondering "what if" and "if only." We have passions and desires to do more things that are bigger than us, but we allow ourselves to be content where we are instead of aiming higher, dreaming larger, and achieving without relent. It's a psychological folly that *AIM High* aims (no pun intended) to correct.

I was in that very same psychological pit, until I'd realized that I had a choice. It's the very same choice that you and everyone else on earth has. We could choose to have a decent life, filled with success based on merit and work. Or, we could have a purposed life, filled with intentional decisions that produce greatness from ourselves and others.

Essentially, we're choosing to be either the land or the laborer. It all comes down to how we define our purpose.

I didn't know how to find my own, at first. I just knew that there was "more." I knew that there were these great ideas and huge dreams to impact the world and leave my footprint, but I had no clue on when, where, or how to start. What I did know, however, was that like anything else worth having, if I was ever going to figure it out, I'd have to put in the work.

I eventually wrote the vision and made myself a vision board. It was essentially another piece of wall decor (poster board) filled with a passionately made collage of all of the things that I'd wanted in my life. It's an effective tool (that I'll get into later). For now, all that's necessary for you to know is that, nothing happened. Needless to say, I was quite disappointed (I'd worked really hard on the project).

For months, I sat stagnant and wondering why— though I could see my vision, it wasn't coming true? It's obvious to me now (likely to you as well), but the answer hit me across the head like the mother of the church who'd caught me chewing gum in church. *I hadn't been actively chasing my goals.* I'd just been languishing in them.

I soon realized *"that faith without works was dead."* It dawned on me that I *"couldn't just hear about faith. I needed to use my faith to hurl myself into action."* Although I am a believer, faith is never

4

the easiest thing to do. Again, I was stuck on what to do next.

One day, I was watching television and I heard someone say, "if you choose not to make a decision, you are still making a decision by not doing anything about it." It hit me, but not immediately, as one would assume.

Weeks passed and I was so afraid of making the wrong decision or choosing to go in the wrong direction, that I let fear keep me stuck in the same place. I let my own lack of faith drive me into stagnancy and dictate my future before I'd even so much as taken the first step.

I was afraid of making the wrong decision and of being wrong, so I made a decision to remain stagnant and stuck, if only to protect myself from my worst fear. In retrospect, it sounds a bit silly but, through experience, you'll find that there are few greater foes than the ones that you come up with in your own head.

This books aims (still no pun intended) to assist you with that particularly troublesome inner battle and the external struggle that befalls all who confidently march toward success.

This blueprint was designed at a point in my life where I didn't want to be stuck. I wanted to be free.

The purpose of sharing "AIM HIGH: Create a Blueprint to Conquer Your Life", is to see Dreams transition to Goals and Goals transition to Manifestation. Ultimately, I hope your vision will inspire someone to live a life that ***PROSPERS OFF OF PURPOSE***.

**AIM**, according to Merriam Webster, means to **direct** a course; specifically: to point a weapon at an object. to aspire; to intend; to direct toward a specified object or goal.

**Direct** means to determine a course or procedure; to regulate activities, and carry out the organizing, energizing, and supervising of something.

A **Blueprint** is a detailed plan or program of action. Usually in the form of maps and architects' plans.

**Create** means to bring into existence.

We were created to create. There are ideas and visions in us that don't exist because we haven't created them. There is something that only you can do. There is a hidden treasure in each of us. There is a unique idea, vision, dream, or goal in each of us that is waiting to come into existence. It only requires us to AIM HIGH.

The vision comes alive when we give it direction. The more we direct the vision to follow a planned course, the stronger the vision becomes. We establish blueprints and detailed plans of action for our visions when we remain consistent in following the course.

During this journey it is vital that you intentionally direct the course of your life. This book requires you to map out your life and create a detailed plan of action. It is designed to challenge your mindset to move from "I don't have enough to start" to "what can I do with the resources I have."

Go, set your sights high, direct the course of the vision with a detailed plan, and remember that your greatest successes still lay ahead of you—so long as you're willing to put in the work.

"Anyone can read and follow directions, but A Visionary creates the directions for others to follow."

## *How to use this book?*

It is best if you follow the book in chronological order initially (as each phase builds on the previous phase). Remember that we are building and creating something that doesn't currently exist, so it's important that you follow through to see its proper manifestation.

The *TYPS* in the book are used to encourage and uplift your inner man, woman, and spirit. Transitioning through the phases of life stir up emotions that can become a distraction if you don't view them through the right lens. "The TYPS will help you avoid emotional and mental pitfalls on your journey."

## *What is a Vision Board?*

The beginning of the year is usually the time to create vision boards. A vision board is a tool used to express your ideas by compiling images that display the life you want or the things you want in life. It is a snapshot of your desires and dreams. Everyone should make a vision board, and be willing to do the work to make their vision a reality.

The vision planning blueprint that you will create will ultimately lead to the creation of a vision board. If you created a vision board and are still waiting to see manifestations, consider starting over, as your current set of goals may not be enough to drive you toward action. It's okay to regularly adjust your vision board.

The idea is to keep you motivated and focused. Some of the ideas on your current vision board may certainly be used for the new one. As you go through this guide, nothing is wasted or thrown away, some ideas will just be moved to a different season, and others to a different year entirely.

It's all about:

## *Efficiency through Attainability*

If it doesn't get you up and going, than quite frankly, it can wait.

# A.I.M High Tool Kit

**Some tools that will be useful to complete this journey:**

Accountability Partner

Bible

Journal

Kleenex for tears

White Paper and Poster Boards

Pens, Pencils, Paper- (vision map)

Deadlines

Calendar- mark dates to coincide with vision
board deadlines

Reward system- (reward should be reasonable to
the task accomplished)

# *Embrace the Vision*

## Accountable to Your Vision

As a visionary, you are responsible for the vision. There are steps that you should take to gain clarity and understanding of the vision you are trying to execute. Often, we place our visions and dreams into the hands of others and allow their thoughts and opinions to change the vision and we get upset when we don't see the results desired.

When this happened, more than likely, somewhere along the way, we became lazy. Before placing your dream and vision into the hands of others there are some necessary questions that you should ask yourself.

For instance, I wanted to start a nonprofit with a focus on mentoring. At the time, I didn't do any research on mentoring programs, I just knew that I wanted to start my own. Most nonprofits are funded through grants and charitable donations. The donations are given based on the need in the community. If there are 10 other non-profits in the same city with similar missions, it can be difficult to convince others to help fund your project.

### *Things I learned along the way:*

1.) **What type of business entity should I use?** I had a LLC at the time, but I had to change the LLC into a 501(c)(3), because people are inclined to give if they can get a tax write off. The thought of the application was intimidating and would require assistance to complete, but I looked at the application anyway. Walking into unfamiliar territory will intimidate us and make us uncomfortable, but being uncomfortable will force us to grow. Eventually, the areas that appeared to be intimidating will become your new norm.

2.) I needed to survey the number of mentoring programs in the city and the population of people they were servicing. I needed to read their platforms and models and research their community projects. This process can be extremely intimidating because it will appear that established businesses/organizations have more to offer... **build anyway**. Always know who is serving alongside you to the same population you want to serve.

3.) I had to ask myself, *"What do I have to offer that these other organizations didn't have?"* "Why was my organization needed, if someone was doing something similar?" Remind yourself that you are valuable. Remind yourself why. Be prepared to encourage yourself and know that the harvest is plentiful but the laborers are few. There is room at the table for you too. It may be similar but it's not the same.

4.) I had to re-evaluate my mission, vision, goals, and objectives to ensure that they were clear. If someone halfway across the world wanted to get involved, would they understand everything from reading a pamphlet, a one page document, or the website? Keep it simple and clear so others that see your vision will understand it and be inspired.

5.) I researched the domain name and all of the websites that offer website services, and created social media accounts that would be relevant to the audience I wanted to reach. Be digitally present and current with the times.

6.) I found 3 organizations: One on a local level, national level, and global level that were doing something similar to what I wanted to do. I had to constantly remind myself of the endless possibilities. Aim High because there is always another level.

7.) I evaluated my strengths, and identified my weaknesses and areas that would require more expertise. Know your weaknesses and strengths and ask for help when needed.

8.) I created a projected budget and timeframe to accomplish each goal. Vision cost. Know the cost to carry out your vision. Don't allow the numbers to intimidate you, but motivate you.

9.) I hired a coach, knowing what I wanted, having ideas on how to get it, and ready to take the vision to the next level.

I researched and gained an understanding of my vision and when I got to a point that I did all that I could do, I hired a coach to get me past the obstacles that I'd either not seen or not known how to overcome.

The goal is to position yourself to have a productive conversation about your goals and with others about them. At the time I hired a coach, I was able to have a productive conversation with the coach because I took the time to learn about what I wanted to do and was never ashamed to ask questions or admit that I didn't know something.

I didn't waste time or money breathing on the phone with a coach saying "I don't know" to every question that was asked. I was honest with myself and I chose a direction to follow. Find yours and STICK TO IT! I can not urge that sentiment enough. The fruitfulness of your relationship with your coach and the quality of the conversation is determined by you and is of the utmost importance.

There is homework on the front end that you should do, and there is homework that will be required from you, by your coach. DO NOT take these assignments lightly. If you do your homework you will see substantial growth and results. With enough work, you will see your focus shift from **"why"** you're doing it to strategies on **"how"** to expand and service greater needs.

Your coach will illuminate your ideas and keep you accountable to your goals. If you're at your best, you will get the best out of your coach. Their job is to assist in your growth, not to do the work for you. It's imperative that you understand and willingly take on the challenges that you will be required to face.

The process of birthing something new is scary. Your coach should be someone that has already cleared the land in the field you desire to enter into, and will be able to guide you to do the same.

## *It's Not Where You Start but How You Finish*

This book is unique because it allows each individual person to create a blueprint for their life according to what is best for them. We come from different upbringings, environments, cultures, countries, religious beliefs, and ethnicities, therefore, we are our own unique vision.

Our differences make us special. Our uniqueness is the reason we should take pride in our story and not attempt to duplicate other's stories for our lives. We can glean the best from those who inspire us and apply the principles that will work for our individual lives.

God made each of us with a particular set of detailed traits. He did not pull us off an assembly line. He took his time to form and fashion us. We can't take the easy way out and follow someone else's blueprint, because our journeys will vary. However, we can take the time and create our own blueprint and trust that our experiences will guide us into developing something great.

I have two friends, Marie and Nicole. They are both Nurse Practitioners. Their routes started from a different place but they finished in the same room. Despite their individual blueprints, the destination was the same.

They were able to accomplish their goals (which happened to be the same) by bearing the weight of their own God-given schematic.

## *Marie:*

Marie and I became friends in seventh grade. As long as I can remember she was determined to be something great. She never wanted to be a product of her environment or another negative statistic.

Marie was street smart, book smart, and always a step ahead of our mutual friends. Marie's name was always on the glass wall of the front office for our quarterly report card conferences. She really loved school, and in the tenth grade I found out why.

Some of my friends were punished because their mom's didn't see their names on the office glass. Marie's name was always on the glass and she always hoped that one day her mom would recognize it. School was her escape.

On the homefront, there were lots of responsibilities given to her and not enough nurturing or encouragement. At school, she formed bonds with certain faculty and staff and was encouraged daily. All of her hard work appeared to be in vain by our junior year when Marie found out she was pregnant.

Discouraged and ashamed, she wanted to drop out and even considered an abortion. It was in the abortion clinic that she recalled her mother didn't abort her as a teenage parent, and her grandmother didn't abort her mother as a teenage parent. After much consideration, she decided to keep the baby.

Marie realized that although she made a similar mistake, she was already making strides on her path that her mother and grandmother had never accomplished. Despite her newfound motherhood, she graduated from high school with honors.

While in high school Marie received her CNA (Certified Nursing Assistant) Certification. After graduating, Marie started working as a CNA for a year. The support from family and friends and her child's father was sporadic, but she remained focused and trusted God.

The following fall semester she enrolled into a nursing program to become a Licensed Practical Nurse (LPN). Marie was a single mother, in school, and on a fixed income, but her drive and work ethic inspired everyone around her. She completed her LPN program, but she was determined to keep going.

Marie worked and saved money for a year before starting her journey to become a Registered Nurse. Witnessing her walk across the stage to receive her BSN, as if it was a cakewalk humbled many people. Instead of complaining about our obstacles we thought "what would Marie do" because she mastered areas in life that people twice our age were still struggling to overcome.

After graduation, Marie took 2 years off from school gained experience, saved money, and helped her daughter acclimate to a new neighborhood and new school. When her 2 years were up, Marie applied and was accepted into graduate school, and graduated on time.

She later continued her studies and all the licensing requirements to become a Nurse Practitioner.

Marie is currently happily married and a Nurse Practitioner—preparing to open clinics in her city and the surrounding areas to service populations in need.

## *Nicole:*

Nicole was "green" and goofy. We also met in seventh grade and are still friends today. She was the friend that was too nice and always wanted to see the good in everyone she met. Nicole's name was also on the glass by the office for report card conference. She was active in many extra-curricular activities in high school.

Nicole was always one step ahead of everyone with her fashionable attire and creativity. She worked with the art and theater department and designed many events and shows. Her family never came to any of the shows or events.

Later, she expressed that her parents always told her, that her creative endeavors were a hobby and she would grow out of it to focus on a real career. Toward the end of our junior year, Nicole was determined to leave Louisiana and attend college out of state to pursue her passion.

After Hurricane Katrina, she left and never moved back. Nicole finished high school at the top of her class and attended undergrad on a full scholarship. Despite her nerve, she was never outspoken. Due to her reservations, in college she was subject to some heartache, disappointment, pressure, and obstacles a step above what she'd faced while in high school.

Nicole always seemed well put together and she always had a plan. We were shocked, when she expressed her parents pressured her to get good grades to get full scholarships and go to medical school all her life.

Yet, Nicole never wanted to go to medical school. She shared how her parents never came to see her name on the glass wall of the front office because they told her, "she was doing what she was supposed to be doing."

Although Nicole was hurt many times from the lack of support, she used those moments to drive her to get to college so she can make her own decisions.

Nicole studied hard in undergrad, she changed her major from pre-med to nursing, followed the curriculum and was accepted into several nursing schools. She received her RN/BSN and worked for the requisite amount of time required to gain experience before applying to graduate school.

Nicole applied to graduate school and graduated on time. She too continued her studies and all of the licensing requirements to become a Nurse Practitioner. Nicole is currently a Nurse Family Practitioner.

Throughout college Nicole also worked as an event coordinator for different clubs, event halls, and organizations. She started her own event planning company to nurture her creative gifts. She is married and expecting her first child and plan to partner with Marie to open clinics in different communities in her state to service those in need.

## *Finishline:*

Nicole and Marie started their journeys from different places and were offered different opportunities based on their circumstances. Nonetheless, they both accomplished their goals.

It is vital that we walk out the path in life carved out for us. We are unique and different, so one way to accomplish a goal will never service all of us. We don't have to imitate every step in another person's life to reach the same goal.

It would be exhausting to compare and attempt to duplicate someone else's life, especially if you don't have their experiences. It is our experience, both good and bad, that drive and motivate us.

Marie grew up in a single parent home and she was able to use her lack of resources as motivation to provide for her family. Nicole grew up in a two parent home with resources but she never wanted to be home, so she used the lack of support  from her parents in her career choice to motivate her to be the best and graduate at the top of all of her classes.

If Marie had allowed the stigma of "being a teenage mother" to fester in her mind, she wouldn't have moved forward. She would have succumbed to the idea that she had to drop out of school, get a job, stay on government assistance, and never go to college.

Instead, she chose to keep her goals ahead of her. If Marie would have compared her journey to Nicole's journey she would have been discouraged because it appeared that Nicole was moving faster and accomplishing her goals faster.

Nicole supported Marie through her journey and was able to offer guidance because she finished first. Today, Marie is able to teach Nicole, who is a new mother, how to manage motherhood and a career, and how to open her own clinics along with other business endeavors because she finished first.

If Nicole attempted to follow Marie's blueprint she would have been unfulfilled because Nicole had the capacity to handle more. Conversely, if Marie had attempted to follow Nicole's blueprint, she would have failed miserably because, although she was smart, she didn't have the extra time necessary to dedicate to school alone.

In a society where social media displays perfect lives and perfect outcomes, it is vital that we stay grounded and true to who we are. Our background and temporary circumstances should not dictate if we accomplish our goals or fulfill our purpose. Most of all, there is no one way to reach a goal or success.

***AIM High*** was written to help people from any walk of life, look at their circumstances, and not get intimidated by what they may lack. AIM High seeks to encourage and motivate individuals to create a blueprint for where they desire to go on their terms.

*It's not where we start but how we finish.*

**Here are examples of some common goals we could hope to achieve. Feel free to create your own list beneath mine.**

1.) I want to grow stronger in my faith
2.) I want to attend or return to school.
3.) I want to buy a house.
4.) I want to start my own business.
5.) I want to lose weight.
6.) I want to spend more time with my family and friends.
7.) I want to travel.

**Now, you try. What are some of your goals?**

1.) ——————————————————————

2.) ——————————————————————

3.) ——————————————————————

4.) ——————————————————————

5.) ——————————————————————

6.) ——————————————————————

7.) ——————————————————————

# Don't Forsake *TYP*- Tilling Your Purpose

The phrase "till the soil" simply means to prepare the soil for seed planting. The act of tilling requires digging, stirring, overturning, and breaking up the soil.

Once the soil is tilled we learn both the good and bad qualities of the soil. We gain insight on where to till and when to till for future crops, and eventually, how to harvest.

TYP sections are for your internal growth. As we attempt to manifest visions and dreams outwardly, we go through various changes, emotions, and feelings inwardly. TYP encourages your inner seeds so as you plant outwardly, you *plant the best of you and not the "rest" of you.*

*When you see a beautiful house, it is usually introduced first by its beautiful landscaping. Before you allow people to explore the inner you the landscaping of your character is met first, so let it be your best.*

I've included TYP sections after each stage in the book because there are some things that can only be learned through experiences. In order to produce any form of crop you must first till the soil.

As I've tilled the soil in my own life, by trying to live out my purpose, I have learned many things and overcame many things. I'm eager to share the lessons learned from overturning the soil in my own purpose.

Tilling the soil also requires plenty of labor. There are obstacles that you will encounter that will attempt to exhaust you, but **keep digging**. Remember that from this labor, a field of dreams will blossom and flourish.

In digging up the old stuff you will find many nutrient treasures that your normal eye may've overlooked. When you see these raw nutrients with your spiritual eyes you'll see that there is purpose for even the smallest nutrient that appears insignificant. These treasures are only found if you keep digging!

The more you expose yourself to the soil the stronger your desire to plant will be. When you are surrounded by anything that can help you grow, if you're ready, it will be like a magnet drawing you in more and more the closer you come to it.

Tilling the soil stirs up your gifts without trying. Your ideas, your dreams, your goals, automatically shift from seeds of thoughts to possibilities. Every moment you entertain the thought of a possibility, you stir up your divine gifts. The only step left is to plant the seed!

There are a few steps to this blueprint that are necessary to bring your vision from ideas and dreams to an accountable plan and timeline.

This guide will help you to bring your vision board alive.

# PHASE 1:

## WRITE THE VISION

*"Write the vision and make it plain on tablets,
That he may run who reads it"*

First, write the vision. During this phase of the project, it's best to write down everything that comes to mind. No matter how big or small, write the entire vision.

Every goal for your life should be written somewhere and the date it came to mind should be next to it. This process has been referred to as a "brain dump," brainstorming, etc.

Clear your mind and get it all out. Once everything is written, breathe. It may seem like a lot, but don't get overwhelmed. The first major step is done.

These are your ideas and dreams, but they are also your benefits. When you get frustrated on the journey and you ask yourself, *"why am I doing this?"* look back at when and how the idea was given. Always keep the dream in front of you.

This step may look like this:

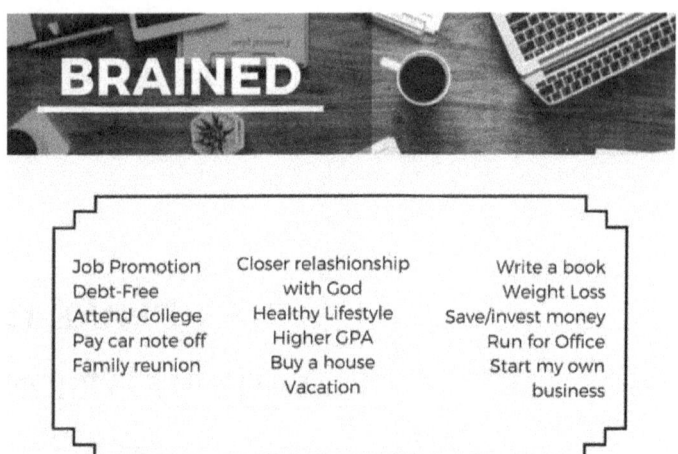

| | | |
|---|---|---|
| Job Promotion | Closer relashionship | Write a book |
| Debt-Free | with God | Weight Loss |
| Attend College | Healthy Lifestyle | Save/invest money |
| Pay car note off | Higher GPA | Run for Office |
| Family reunion | Buy a house | Start my own |
| | Vacation | business |

Next, you're going to take your ideas or goals and categorize them.

First, categorize based on the time frame that you have allotted yourself to accomplish the goal. For example, a five-year goal and a six-month goal would go under different categories. Now, if a part of the five-year goal takes six-months to accomplish, that part of the goal should be with other six-month goals.

Let's use one of the goals I presented in the beginning. The goal in number three is to buy a house. First, I would like to reduce some of my debt. If I have a substantial amount of debt ($100K), it may take a longer period of time to tackle that big of a task. However, after I review my credit report, I may find a smaller financial goal to conquer within a year. If I review my credit report, I may choose a smaller financial goals to conquer within a year. For instance,

I may have $5,000 left on my car note, instead of paying it off in two years I can make a commitment to pay it off in one year. Everything should be done with reasonableness.

If you are $100,000 in debt and you make $75,000 a year, it's not realistic to pay the debt off in one year. Sometimes we place unrealistic expectations on ourselves which lead to pressure, fear, and anxiety when we don't accomplish everything we set out to do. The goals should be categorized according to time. This will prevent unrealistic expectations and keep you from feeling unproductive or like a failure.

This is an estimate based on the information you know today. Some goals will take less time while other goals will take more time. If you begin to research and find that the goal will take a substantial amount of time to complete, don't throw it away.

Assess what has been accomplished thus far and if there are small steps that can be taken toward progress. Continue to take the small steps. If the goal requires more resources and time than your capacity, keep all of the work together and put it in a safe place and you can return to it when the timing is right. ***Timing is everything***.

Here's an example of what you may have:

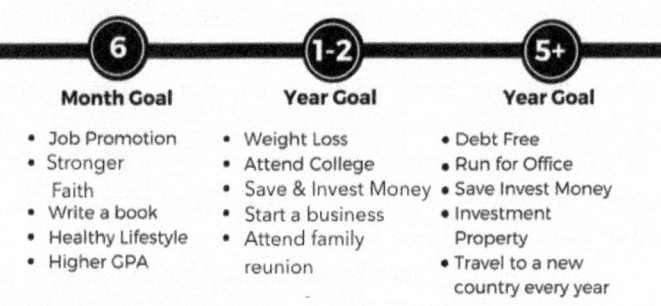

**GOALS CATEGORIZED**

| 6 Month Goal | 1-2 Year Goal | 5+ Year Goal |
|---|---|---|
| • Job Promotion | • Weight Loss | • Debt Free |
| • Stronger Faith | • Attend College | • Run for Office |
| • Write a book | • Save & Invest Money | • Save Invest Money |
| • Healthy Lifestyle | • Start a business | • Investment Property |
| • Higher GPA | • Attend family reunion | • Travel to a new country every year |

*Organizational Idea: A drawer or container system can be used for your different goals and the paperwork for those goals.*

Next, we will categorize the goals based on significance. What are the dreams that you are ready to commit to now? COMMIT is the key word. Categorize your goals based on what's important to you now.

For example, number five on my goal list, *to lose weight*, may be important if I'm taking high blood pressure medication because if I lose 30 pounds I can stop taking the medication. I will be a healthier person, have fewer doctor visits, save money from health care and medications as well as have more time to devote to other activities, etc.. Suddenly, this simple task becomes vastly more important, as its benefits are now clear and I can properly gage its importance against everything else.

It's vital to narrow your goals down to around 5-10 per year. Of course, if it's ten small things that can be accomplished within a three to six-month time frame, more items can be added. However, if it's ten big goals that will make you uncomfortable and will challenge and stretch you all year long, you may be setting yourself up for failure. Don't over do it.

When we look at the list of goals and analyze that the original timeframe or age we wanted to accomplish the goal has passed we may go into panic mode. The question "where do you see yourself three, five, or seven years from now" was asked to ignite a desire to accomplish something, not to scare you off of your path.

If you realize you're behind your schedule, forgive yourself and keep moving. Don't try to do everything at one time because you're trying to "catch up" to your plan. If we over book, over schedule, and drain ourselves we will burn out and nothing will get accomplished. If nothing gets accomplished, we end up back at square one. Pace yourself.

For my example, I'm going to use five of my goals listed above, because when you start to make changes you may only be able to tackle less than you'd intended, and that is okay.

I have written all of my ideas, I have categorized the ideas based on time and importance, and I have selected a few goals that I am ready to tackle this year.

Phase 1 is complete! Do a happy dance. Some people get overwhelmed and never make it pass this phase.

## <u>Tilling Your Purpose In Faith</u>

### TYP – Maintaining along the way, are you prepared?

We start journeys on fire and ready to conquer the world and the moment that the ball starts rolling we are caught off guard by the consistent momentum. We have to prepare for the good, bad, and ugly. Most of all we have to be "prepared." At any moment the vision that you see as small and easy or "*not a big deal*" can become a really big deal. Are you ready for your idea to become a big deal?

The first time I applied to law school I did not get accepted because I wasn't prepared. I did the bare minimum required for the applications and I was upset when I didn't get accepted. Later, I realized that i didn't properly prepare.

The next time I applied to law school, I was accepted. Yet, I still wasn't prepared for the drastic lifestyle changes that were required for me to finish successfully. The first year went by so fast it made my head spin.

Before I knew it, I was leaving my first clerkship and on a plane to London for the entire summer. Everything was overwhelming, because I didn't consider the opportunities that would be afforded to me so quickly.

While I had access to many opportunities, I missed several opportunities because I was trying to juggle personal life, law school, ministry, friendships/relationships and everything else. Initially, in that season, I wasn't prepared to put many things on hold to accomplish the goal I set.

It was after stumbling through my first year, moving to another state for 6 months of the second year that I came up with a plan to stay focused and accountable on the goal of completing law school.

As you seek the manifestation of your ideas, prepare yourself to receive the blessing.

# PHASE 2:

## THE SACRIFICE

*"Faith without works is dead."*

According to **dictionary.com,** sacrifice means to, "surrender or give up, or permit injury or disadvantage to, for the sake of something else."

This is the moment we move from fairytale to reality. In this phase, you will determine if your idea or dream is just fantasy or something actionable. Here, we will determine if you really want it. If you're not willing to sacrifice for it right now, it shouldn't be included in your vision planning at this time.

Everything we do successfully requires a sacrifice of time and resources. Here, you will realize your level of commitment to the vision. After you write down the sacrifices required to accomplish this goal, you may determine if you are ready to take on the task.

This part of the process is very important. There are long term goals we all desire but the time to pursue them and the willingness on our end to accomplish them are necessary for a desired outcome.

During this process, some goals may not get accomplished this time around and that's okay. Place them in your box of treasures and save them for later. Part of the work is done and when the timing is right you can revisit them in earnest.

Significance is also key here. It's vital that we don't singularly pursue the things that will make us feel good. At times, we have to do what we know is needed but may not give us that sense of instant gratification (such as a balanced diet or exercising). Learn to be honest with yourself about what's necessary.

If you have illnesses like high blood pressure, high cholesterol, diabetes that only require some lifestyle changes, add it to your vision and pursue their success as quickly as possible. Nothing is a better motivator than achievement. Small victories, such as a change of diet, can do wonders for your spirit and keep you going, even when things get tough.

With these changes, it also becomes important to address your language. Remember to stay positive in your endeavors and leave little room for negativity to rear its ugly head in your plans. Get ahead of the pessimism by making small tweaks to the way that you think and speak about what you're doing.

Instead of saying, "If I work on my diabetes or high blood pressure I will have to eat unseasoned, flavorless food" choose to say, "I'm excited about developing a healthier lifestyle, pretty soon I won't have to take medication and risk not being here to see my loved ones." View your sacrifice as a symbol of progress and sign that you're finally taking action.

Now let's dive into the things that you're ready to sacrifice for. I'll use my list of five goals that I started with in the beginning.

Your list should look something like this:

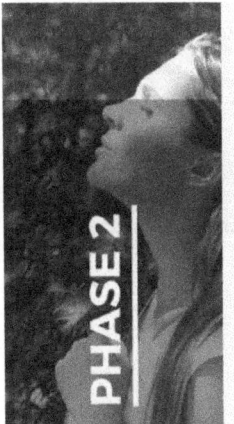

**Bigger Faith and Closer Relationship**

A. Prioritize Time- Create a Daily Schedule
B. Start with 15 minutes every day in the morning and at night
C. After the first month, I'll increase my time in increments of 15 minutes
D. Prayer, Worship, Meditation during this time
E. By 6 months spend one Saturday a month from morning until noon
F. Join or become active in a ministry or volunteer organization
G. Follow network of other leaders in this particular area

**Attend College**

A. Research the colleges that I am interested in attending and review the curriculum for my intended major
B. Call the Enrollment/Admissions Office to get information about admission requirements for at least 3 universities.
C. Setup a time to visit the school and meet with someone in the department of my intended major.
D. Financial Aid- Complete FAFSA application, Inquire about scholarships, grants
E. Housing- Consider the cost of living on campus and off campus.

### I want to purchase a house

**A.** Contact a real estate agent.

**B.** Obtain credit report from a viable source.

**C.** Take the necessary steps recommended by the financial advisor to improve credit, if necessary.

**D.** Attend first home buyer classes and research other grants with my agent.

**E.** Save money by sacrificing unnecessary purchases.

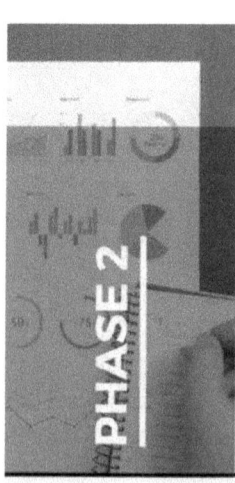

### I want to start my own business

**A.** Create a Name

**a.** Vision, Mission, Purpose, Objectives

**B.** Research/ attend free business classes offered by organizations or universities near you.

**a.** Research Business Information to determine the type of business you want, such as an LLC, Non-Profit, Partnership, Corporation, etc.

**b.** Research whether your product needs to have a Trademark or Copyright protection.

**c.** Are you offering a service or selling products- clothing or classes

**d.** Consider your Audience and who will benefit from product and service

**e.** Conduct Cost Analysis- how much will it cost to start up

**f.** Complete a basic business proposal- who, what, why, when, how, and cost

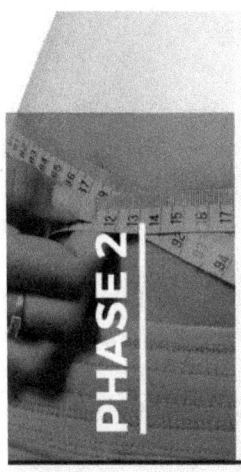

**I want to lose weight**

- Decide what I can do to make a lifestyle change
- Prep meals instead of eating out
- Choose healthier food options
- Proper intake of water everyday
- Eat healthier snacks
- Exercise
- Walk once a day
- Use the stairs instead of the elevator
- Hire a fitness trainer
- Join a gym

PHASE 2

Take a break! We went from high gear excited and ready, to looking at all that will be required to get it accomplished and now we may be a bit dazed. And that's just some of the stuff we have to do. It's not including the bumps in the road. Let's breath and take a ten-minute break.

We have most of the sacrifices listed. Now, let's count the cost.

Some of us may feel that this is possible and it is easier than we thought. We are ready. While others may feel unsure. It seemed like an easy task in the beginning but now it seems to be more overwhelming, right?

# *DON'T PANIC!*

For those people that feel overwhelmed, go through your list again. It's okay to place a few things on hold for this season. Like I'd previously stated, don't throw the work away. Place it in a safe place and you will know when it's time to return to it.

We are not recommending removing things from the list because we don't want to do the work and are lazy. We are carefully considering all of the factors in our lives, such as our families, current obligations, responsibilities, time, and resources.

I'll be honest, for your major goals, the timing will never be right. If you're waiting for the stars to align in your favor, you will be waiting forever. If you've grown accustomed to putting things on hold, hoping and wishing that your schedule will just miraculously open up to accomplish your goals, now is the time to alleviate yourself of that weakness.

You must learn to prioritize your life in a manner that will revolve around your dreams.

*Stop making your dreams adjust to your life, and start making your life adjust to your dreams.*

I know, it sounds easier than it looks. This section is called sacrifice for that reason. Some activities that you enjoy will receive less of your time so your dream can live. Don't be afraid to put your hobbies on the backburner. They'll be there when you get back. For now, you've got too much work to do to be stagnant.

Please go through your list one final time after reviewing the sacrifices for each of your goals.

If you made it through Phase 2, you are too far invested to turn back now. At this point you are all in. Pat yourself on the back, you have survived your worst critic, You!

## <u>Tilling Your Purpose in Fear</u>

*"This vision is too big for me! Let me give this idea to someone else! People will not like it!*
*What if I didn't really hear from God!"* –
<u>*STOP*</u> *and Breathe!!!*

God has not given us a spirit of fear but of power, love, and a sound mind. It took years for me to really embrace this process of developing this material. I was afraid that people wouldn't like it or that they would think it was unnecessary.

I was afraid that like other ventures, this too would fail. One day while talking to some of my college professors they shared their stories of how they failed over and over again, but refused to quit. I took that advice, and whenever I got discouraged I said to myself, "If you get up you won't regret it later."

I graduated from law school and was prepared to take the first part of the Louisiana State Bar Exam, The Professional Responsibility Exam. I studied but I used the wrong method. My friend who was my study partner throughout law school is extremely smart. I studied the same amount of time as her and used some of her methods. When I went to take the exam I fell asleep.

When I woke up, I started answering the exam questions as quickly as I could within the little time remaining. Unsurprisingly, I failed. Of course, my friend passed with flying colors. Throughout law school she learned everything fast. It was no surprise that she passed. I'm smart but I knew I required more time and effort to achieve something that came so easy to her.

This exam made me fear the second part of the Bar Exam—which is 21 hours over the course of 3 days, the longest Bar Exam in the country. I studied hard and worked hard because I did not want to fail. I passed part 2 of the Bar Exam, which is notorious for its difficulty, but I still had to pass the first part.

I'd conquered one of the hardest bar exams in the country and was still afraid to take the easiest part. I never really failed at anything concerning school my whole life so the thought of taking the exam again and failing again brought lots of anxiety.

I conquered the fear when I evaluated what I did right and what I could've done differently. As I reflected, I realized that I didn't properly prepare. I rearranged my study regiment to model the study schedule I used for part 2 of the exam.

I put the same energy and dedication from part 2 of the exam into part 1 and I passed. If I had allowed the test to intimidate me, I would still be stuck on the sidelines. Don't allow fear of failure to keep you stuck. Get up and get in the game!

## *Keep Your "Why" In Front of You*

"What if it's not about the test?" said a faint voice in one of the most stressful weeks of my life. It was a late evening on Thursday, February 23, 2017, and I was sitting in my office/study room at home when I heard those words that led my emotions to a place of anger, frustration, confusion, and feeling slightly defeated.

Surrounded by books, laptops, binders, and study snacks, I couldn't believe that for the last 4 months I had been preparing for this week of testing, and God was preparing me for something greater.

Initially, when I heard those words, out of frustration I immediately pushed the thoughts to the back of my mind and returned to my studies. My last test was only hours away and I refused to entertain random moments.

Shortly after the test, I assessed my mental, spiritual, emotional, and physical state, and realized that I was in bad shape. I allowed the test to consume me, so much so, there was a decline in every aspect of my life.

I was so determined to pass the test that I was willing to sacrifice everything for it. There were different moments when I felt my body shut down but I pleaded with God to allow me to study anyway.

Several of my conversations went like this, "Lord, just keep me alive until I take the test, if I'm sick or something is wrong, just let me take the test and I'll deal with my health later."

I wanted a doctorate degree because I was the first-generation college student on both sides of my family. I truly desired to shift an entire bloodline and lineage on both sides. My siblings, cousins, and generations to come will never have the notion of generational curses hanging over their head.

They would know that they could obtain any level of education desired if they wanted it. I knew my story would become so many others story. I knew that I would be assigned as a changing agent to offer grace in a system of merciless laws.

In the beginning, I knew it was purposeful and I saw the bigger picture.

I enjoyed learning and understanding the law, but I didn't love it. Yet, I was willing to risk everything for it. What was I really fighting for? And after passing the test, would that be enough? Or would I feel the need to fight for the best job, best position? And after reaching the peak in my career, would that be enough? What was really my goal? And did I have the right perspective of achieving it? Initially, it was Kingdom Centered and I really wanted to help people. But was it still Kingdom Centered? Or did I lose my focus on the purpose of the assignment?

As all of these questions raced through my mind I recognized that I needed a tune up or tune in. My lifeline was very flat. It had no heartbeat, it had no rhythm. I started to desire a place that would never bring fulfillment to my life. A road that would keep me searching for the next best thing, but never being truly content.

It was a desire of my heart, based on the condition of my heart at the time. My desire for worldly success and the willingness to sacrifice so much to get there distorted my perspective of my assignment.

When we are in the marketplace there is consistent pressure to desire marketplace success rather than fulfill purposeful assignments. Despite being surrounded by friends and colleagues that are assigned to do something different, we can't afford to lose focus of the purpose and plan.

We are supposed to be changing agents in the marketplace, and not allow the marketplace to change or redirect us from the purpose of the assignment. We must be careful to protect what we hear through conversations, see in boardrooms and meetings, so that we are aware but not conformed.

When I began to delight myself in God, my heart desires changed. The desired outcome of my work shifted from self-centered and self-accomplishments to God centered Kingdom accomplishments.

The measurement of my success changed from numbers and positions and salaries to the number of lives changed that will change more lives. My skill set, knowledge, and tools gained from my education and experience in the marketplace will still be used but my success will be evaluated using a different perspective.

Sometimes we get absorbed in trying to overcome the test. We get lost in wanting to win the battle that we forget why we are fighting and what we are fighting for.

Our creator is so gracious that even when we lose sight, He still allows all of the circumstances to work together for our good. I thought preparing for this test would solidify a lifelong goal, but it actually prepared me to fulfill my purpose.

*Are you fighting for something?*
*Is it worth fighting for?*

# PHASE 3:

## DECREE AND DECLARE POSITIVE AFFIRMATIONS

*"Life and death are in the power of your tongue..."*
*Proverbs 18:21*

*"As a man thinks in his heart, so is he..."*
*Proverbs 23:7*

This phase is to silence the small voice that attempts to discourage you and tell you to give up and throw in the towel.

There will be moments that you will feel sucker punched on your journey. Moments where your head will spin. Either life will throw you a fast ball OR God's favor will fall so heavy in progressing your vision that it will leave you in awe.

In a good head spin, don't get comfortable, you will need to continue to decree or declare greatness over your vision. The momentum from a good head spin can catapult you into the next phase of your vision. Ride this wave of momentum.

In a bad head spin, you will have to enforce that greatness that lies within the core of your vision, regardless of what happened.

It's best to memorize some of these affirmations for those moments when you're in meetings with unfavorable results and conversations with unhealthy criticism. This phase is preparing you for the moments that will be the life or death to your goal.

When you hit a stumbling block, negative encounter, or sluggish attitude, you will make a decision to press on and keep going or sit on the side lines. I'm hoping that you press beyond your trials and tribulations. The best way to overcome opposition and adversity is to prepare for it even before it comes.

Have you ever worked on any of your goals in the past and didn't succeed? This is the time to replay the tape from the last experience. What happened on the field? Study your actions and study your opponent's actions? How did your opponent succeed? How could you have won the battle? Your opponent may be doubt, fear, insecurities, friends, family, others, etc. Your goal is to look back and recall what was said, what was done, and what made you give up?

Write those things down. I know it can be hurtful, but push through the pain. If you can't face those things now, you won't be able to face them again later.

Write the stumbling blocks down.

_____

_____

_____

_____

_____

_____

Now, for those people who have never attempted to achieve these goals, if you wanted to sabotage your dreams and goals, what would _you_ do to _you_? What would _you_ say to _you_?

Write those things down.

_____

_____

_____

_____

_____

_____

## STUMBLING BLOCKS

- You never complete anything.
- Your products cost too much.
- When are you going to get a real job?
- No one is going to support you.
- Everyone is doing the same thing.
- You finally have your "lil" business.
- Are you going to give a family/ friend discounts?

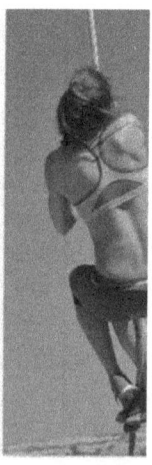

Now that we know what can stop us from winning, let's create a plan that can help us win. In sports, before a game, the teams study their personal mistakes and successful tactics from previous games. The teams also study their opponent's mistakes and successful tactics.

Studying the other team mistakes reveal their weak spots. If we know their weak spot, we can attack that area specifically because the opposing team has not properly mastered that area.

Studying the other teams successful tactics reveal their mastered areas. If we are aware of a successful tactic, we are able to intervene and dismantle it because we know their next move.

This is exactly how the enemy thinks when he is preparing to sabotage our visions. We have to strategize and stay one step ahead of him. He uses the same tactics all the time, he never comes up with anything new. We have to study his moves like he studies our moves. As Bishop Carmen Bazile would say, "You have to know how to sneak a devil." You have to beat him at his own game.

The exercise, that I just asked you to do, was solely to find out your weak spots. Now that you know your weak spots, you can properly secure those areas and when the opposition comes against you, you will already be guarded and prepared. As one of my mentors would say, "You will be able to take a licking and keep on ticking."

Now that we have identified the weak spots, let's guard and secure them with positive affirmations and declarations. We need strategy for offense and defense.

In this phase, you also want to identify two people that you know who have accomplished this goal. One that you know personally, and another person that you've never met but admire, such as a celebrity or public figure that have shared their story.

Let's begin finding our affirmations. I'm still using my same list of goals from the beginning.

### Bigger Faith and Closer Relationship

**A.** Psalm 23:1
The Lord is my shepherd, I have all that I need.

**B.** Isaiah 54:17
No weapon formed against me shall prosper.

**C.** Romans 8:28
And we know that God causes everything to work together for the good of those who love God and are called according to his purpose for them.

Someone that I know personally
my grandmother

Person I admire from a distance
Dr. Myles Munroe

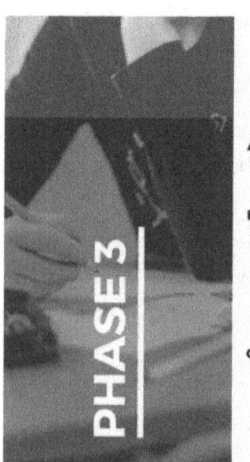

### I want to attend or return to school

**A.** Philippians 4:13
I can do all things through Christ who strengthens me

**B.** Isaiah 40: 30-31
Those who trust in the Lord will find new strength. They will soar high on wings like eagles. They will run and not grow weary. They will walk and not faint.

**C.** Deuteronomy 31:8
Do not be afraid or discouraged, for the Lord will personally go ahead of you. He will be with you; he will neither fail you nor abandon you."

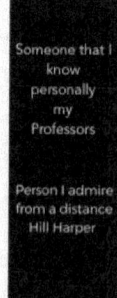

Someone that I know personally
my Professors

Person I admire from a distance
Hill Harper

## I want to buy a house

**A.** Joshua 1:3
Every place that the sole of your foot will tread upon I have given you

**B.** Philippians 4:19
And my God shall supply all your need according to His riches in glory by Christ Jesus.

**C.** Isaiah 32:18
My people will live in peaceful dwelling places, in secure homes, in undisturbed places of rest

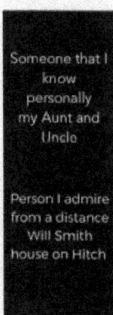

Someone that I know personally my Aunt and Uncle

Person I admire from a distance Will Smith house on Hitch

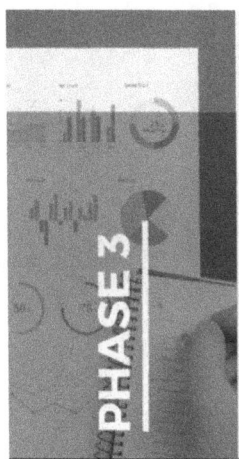

## I want to start my own business

**A.** Philippians 1:6
being confident of this, that he who began a good work in you will carry it on to completion until the day of Christ Jesus

**B.** Deuteronomy 28:12-13
The Lord will open the heavens, the storehouse of his bounty, to send rain on your land in season and to bless all the work of your hands. You will lend to many nations but will borrow from none. The Lord will make you the head, not the tail. If you pay attention to the commands of the Lord your God that I give you this day and carefully follow them, you will always be at the top, never at the bottom.

Someone that I know personally SIAMS Mentor

Person I admire from a distance Oprah Winfrey

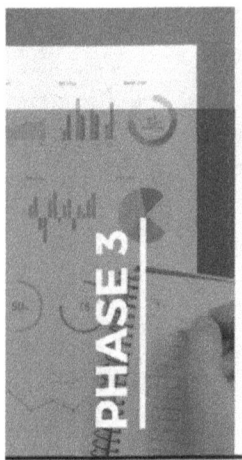

## I want to start my own business

**A.** Philippians 1:6

being confident of this, that he who began a good work in you will carry it on to completion until the day of Christ Jesus

**B.** Deuteronomy 28:12-13

The Lord will open the heavens, the storehouse of his bounty, to send rain on your land in season and to bless all the work of your hands. You will lend to many nations but will borrow from none. The Lord will make you the head, not the tail. If you pay attention to the commands of the Lord your God that I give you this day and carefully follow them, you will always be at the top, never at the bottom.

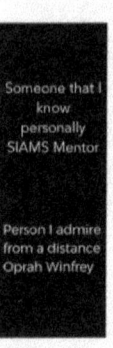

Someone that I know personally
SIAMS Mentor

Person I admire from a distance
Oprah Winfrey

## I want to lose weight

**A.** Psalm 40:1-2

I waited patiently for the Lord; he turned to me and heard my cry. He lifted me out of the slimy pit, out of the mud and mire; he set my feet on a rock
and gave me a firm place to stand.

**B.** Romans 12:1

offer your bodies as a living sacrifice, holy and pleasing to God—this is your true and proper worship.

**C.** Psalm 32:8

I will instruct you and teach you in the way you should go;
I will counsel you with my loving eye on you.

Someone that I know personally
my cousin lost 150 pounds

Person I admire from a distance
Jennifer Hudson

# PHASE 3

# LIST OF AFFIRMATIONS AND QUOTES

FOOD FOR THOUGHT

*It always seems impossible, until it's done!*

-Nelson Mandela

At this stage, get excited! We have successfully conquered three phases. The hardest phases are two and three because they make you address the parts that most people prefer to skip.

Now you can sing your fight song. If you don't have one, think of the song that picks you all the way up when you feel all the way down. Listen to your fight song. If you have more than one, that's great, make a playlist!

Here are a few of my fight songs:
1) I'm Every Woman- Chaka Khan
2) I'm Getting Ready- Tasha Cobbs Leonard
3) Beautiful- Mali Music

## LIST OF AFFIRMATIONS AND QUOTES

**YOU SHOULD SET GOALS BEYOND YOUR REACH SO YOU ALWAYS HAVE**

SOMETHING TO LIVE FOR

TED TURNER

BE STUBBORN ABOUT YOUR GOALS BUT

FLEXIBLE

ABOUT YOUR METHODS

Motivation is what gets you started

# HABIT

is what keeps you going.

-Jim Rohn

## TYP- Tilling your purpose in Disbelief

*"Lord I believe, help my disbelief."*

Most of my earlier projects didn't jumpstart because I didn't believe in them. God will send others that believe in your vision so that you can see the purpose in it and start believing too.

I read the bible, studied the bible, had many words from God spoken over my life but still felt fruitless. It's not a good place to sit. When you have fertile soil, good seed, the right farming tools, in the right season, and still refuse to plant the crop because you don't believe that they will grow, you have a big problem.

There are other times when you know the seeds will grow but you don't believe the harvest will be big enough to make an impact. Any harvest, big or small, represents life. God creates life. If he gave life to your harvest whether big or small it can be used.

Jesus used two fish and five loaves and multiplied them to feed thousands. God wants to do the same with you. First, you have to believe that the God on the inside of you is worth planting.

One day I was sitting and thought to myself, "you're reading and studying and you're feeling good but do you even believe in this word of God, do you receive it?" You can be afraid, but you absolutely must believe. There's a fine line between the two.

Until you believe that God can accomplish this assignment through you, it will never take off the way it was intended. You might fall and you will make mistakes, but you have to know that no matter what happens God's word will still manifest.

Whether you have 5 seeds or 100 seeds, plant the seed, and God will send others to help you water and nurture them.. The boy gave Jesus his two fish and five loaves, which is impossible to feed so many people, but when it was placed in Jesus' hands it multiplied to an abundance.

Every seed of an idea you plant and place in God hands will multiply!

## *Unbelief*

"Lord, I believe, help my unbelief!" (Mark 9:23-25) Unbelief stopped me from producing 3 projects.

The first project was HAIR. I absolutely love hair! After years of spending lots of money on hair, the opportunity to be a vendor presented itself. I was eager to be a vendor of the quality of hair I used personally, because I believed in the brand.

I prayed for God to increase and grow my clientele and he did. As business grew I asked God to allow this supplemental income to increase so I didn't have to work, and He did. I was attending graduate school at night and volunteering for matters that really touched my heart during the day.

The quality of the product sold itself, so I did very little advertising. During this time, many people sold hair and marketed hair products, but in spite of the numerous vendors, locally and nationally, God continued to increase my customers.

After months of this business being my primary income I began to look into other ways to expand. Shortly after, I was contacted by my supplier that the family business was dividing the business and I needed to choose which family member would be my supplier. This phone call confused me.

I was afraid to pick the wrong supplier and risk selling a product of less quality to my customers. I was confused and discouraged. I chose not to work with either of them and to stop working on the business altogether.

A few months later, I met a lady that was building her hair business. We connected through a faith based organization. She wasn't knowledgeable nor did she have a love for hair, but she saw it as a profitable business move, and it was.

I began to share my knowledge and assist her to bring her vision to pass. It started off small but through prayer and faith it took off. And after talking with God, he later revealed that I could've had the same opportunity but I didn't fight for it and I didn't seek him.

I forgot that God had given it to me, He honored a request and desire of my heart, He increased it and multiplied it, and I didn't even seek Him before I gave it all up.

When God gives us insight to accomplish something, it's best that we always seek His face and approval throughout the entire process. Many of us start with a vision or opportunity given by God and we make the mistake of allowing worldly wisdom and advice from others to steer the process. The moment God is removed from the pilot seat, the moment you make your business vulnerable and susceptible to worldly results, you have forsaken your blessing.

Although I was hurt when God gave the revelation that I could've had access to the same opportunities, I enjoyed helping another sister in Christ accomplish her goal. We can't allow the hurt and pain from our failures and disappointments to keep us from spreading the knowledge and wisdom we gained from the experience.

It may not have worked in my favor, but the wisdom will not be wasted. It makes no sense to endure pain and not reap a harvest. The harvest may not be of monetary value but may come in the form of someone else growing and glowing. If life calls for you to be a match to help someone else's light shine, please extend the help.

# PHASE 4:

## MY RESOURCES

*"I will supply all of your needs according to my riches and glory."*

### re·source
**ˈrēˌsôrs,rəˈsôrs/**
*noun*

1. a stock or supply of money, materials, staff, and other assets that can be drawn on by a person or organization in order to function effectively.

We can't accomplish anything in this world alone. There is always someone who will have more access, expertise, wisdom, knowledge, funds, and connections. Knowing the resources that are currently available to you can prevent you from spending unnecessary money and wasting time.

For instance, attending school. If you know a family member, friend, church member, organization, or community program that has enrolled and graduated from a university, consider talking to them about enrolling or returning to school.

If you know your intended major, you can reach out to individuals that are currently in the profession that you're interested in. At worst, they may possibly know someone that is.

If you don't know an individual personally, consider going to a school with your desired major and talking to an admissions counselor or professor in that department. The more knowledge and information you can obtain, the more peace you will have in making your decisions.

Sometimes we overlook the obvious resources that are readily available to us. Spend a few minutes thinking about your goal and all the people that may be able to assist you. If you're unsure or don't have any one that can assist, begin to search for organizations and community programs in your city that can be beneficial.

Do you have the skill set needed? Sometimes we are limited in our ability because we don't have the skill set. This is not a reason to abort the mission. There may be a goal or dream that is totally out of your field. You may be limited in knowledge, but utilize connections and networking in that field.

Don't shy away from a goal or dream because it's not in your field. Find the experts in the area and get the job done.

I was working on a project in regard to counseling and its totally not in my field. However, I knew people that were in the field and with their help, we made it happen.

## *Strengths vs. Weaknesses*

*What are you capable of doing? What type of expertise is needed to accomplish the goal?*

Most of all, always remember your primary source, which is God. There are some things that networking and connections won't be able to do. It's always important to keep your silent partner, God, in the conversation. He can direct your path, order your steps, give you favor, and create opportunities that man cannot.

An example of your resource page should like this:

**PHASE 4
WRITING A
BOOK**

**What I can do**

Write the manuscript
Create social media pages
Photo shoot
Buy my domain name
Create my own website
Prepare material for
workshops
Book possible speaking
engagements

**What I need**

Publisher – contact self publishing coaches
Editor- contact 2 from writers workshop
Graphic Designer- contact the person that
worked on SN book
Marketing and branding- contact the lady
from journey conference
Photographer- use the guy from
graduation
Focus group- ask 10 women (work, church,
school)
Title- get feedback from focus group

## <u>TYP Tilling Your Purpose while Shifting- Move when God says move.</u>

We are always learning something new. Some of us are certified, have degrees, or some level of expertise in certain areas of our lives. We also have experiences and other methods to gather information and knowledge.

Still, there will be times when God will ask us to do something that can't be traced back to a book or experience. It simply won't make sense or add up. We must move or shift anyway. We have to trust God through the entire process.

Hesitating or failing to move can cost you more than staying where you are. When God speaks move on His timing. He is able to see what's coming ahead and prepare you for the valley or mountain top experience. Some opportunities don't come back around. Some doors will close and not open again. More Importantly, the people He will use you to bless lives depend on your obedience in the move.

If God gave you a vision or dream or goal, and He has made provisions, opened doors, allowed you to connect etc. Please know that God has a strategy to carry it all the way through. Failing to seek God in the beginning and leaning on your own understanding is a recipe for failure.

*"Proper planning prevents poor performance. Poor performance is due to poor preparation."*

There is nothing worse than having an opportunity and being unprepared for it. Once you start working on these ideas, resources will find you and conversations will include you. You will have an awareness in everything you do and become intentional in all of your conversations. Don't let your opportunity present itself and be forced to decline the very thing you prayed for because you were not prepared.

# PHASE 5:

## DEADLINES

*"Good planning and hard work lead to prosperity,
but hasty shortcuts lead to poverty."*

Deadlines are our first accountability partners. Too often we fail to uphold deadlines for our personal goals. However, when it comes to work, family, and other endeavors we keep hard deadlines.

The same discipline used to complete our work assignments and other endeavors is necessary to complete the personal goals you desire to accomplish. We can't accomplish anything with a "someday" or "one day" mentality.

Deadlines are necessary. One step we can take to ensure that deadlines are easier to complete is breaking a goal into a few steps. In doing this, we simplify a seemingly impossible task into much smaller and more attainable obstacles.

For instance, if you're working on weight loss, you may choose to meal prep. It may take four hours to meal prep for the entire week. Sunday may be your only free day. If so, you may want to use it for family time and relaxing.

Instead of spending 4 hours of this day to prep for the week, you can spend 2 hours on Sunday and 2 hours on another day in the week. The goal will be accomplished, but it won't be overwhelming and take away from your family.

Another example is someone trying to go back to school. Just the thought of returning to school can be intimidating. This goal can be broken up. One day you may want to spend time looking and comparing majors and curriculums between schools. Another day you can spend time sending emails and calling the institutions that most interest you. Finally, you can complete college applications for the universities that will best serve the needs of your intended goals.

Most times, we try to block out an entire work day, eight hours, and accomplish everything in that day. For some people that will work. For others, that may not be as effective. Of course, your method will be determined by the other obligations and responsibilities in your life.

The intimidation is removed when you take on a task in small bites. Every goal, subpart of a goal, must have an intended deadline or end date.

Always calibrate your dates. If you miss a deadline, recalibrate your date without disturbing other deadlines, unless absolutely necessary.

Calendars are your second accountability partners. Once every goal has been assigned a deadline, the next step is to mark them on our calendars.

Technology has made life a lot easier and we can have access to our calendars all the time through electronic devices. Before we place the deadlines in our phone calendars, we will place them on our physical calendars.

Studies have shown that we remember more of what we see than what we hear or read. Every morning your calendar should be visible in an area where your eyes can be fixated on it. Your phone will remind you during the course of your day that a big day is approaching.

**May 2018** → **Buying a House Deadlines**

**PHASE 5 WRITE DOWN DEADLINES IN NOTEBOOK AND PLACE DEADLINES ON CALENDAR**

| | | | | | | |
|---|---|---|---|---|---|---|
| | | 1 Call agent | 2 | 3 | 4 | 5 Meet with agent |
| 6 | 7 | 8 | 9 | 10 | 11 | 12 Attend first homebuyers class |
| 13 | 14 | 15 | 16 | 17 | 18 | 19 Attend 1st homebuyer class |
| 20 | 21 | 22 | 23 | 24 | 25 Pay off $300 bill | 26 |
| 27 | 28 | 29 | 30 | 31 Setup payment plans for debt collector | | |

## **TYP - Tiling Your Purpose in Doubt**

Are you qualified? Of course not! We're all unqualified in our own right to work with God. But that's what makes it such an honor. He uses unqualified people all the time, so that He can get the glory.

However, God doesn't work with everybody. If He chose you to work with him in any capacity, that's huge, because it's God. What's even better, is knowing that God can create someone who can do it exactly how it needs to be done, but he still chooses us and allows us to get on the job training.

God never uses people that have it all together because the glory will go to the individual instead of God. God is a jealous God, He won't let anyone steal the credit for His work. Are you the person for the job? Of course, you are! God doesn't make mistakes.

His word never returns to him void. He has to use you to confuse everyone that doubted you. He has to use you because they will have to acknowledge God's greatness when they see you got the job done.

I was in law school and wanted to apply for an externship to work at Texas State Capitol for six months. It's a very competitive program. The day I started working on the application, I saw some of my peers that were smarter, had higher GPA's, and spoke very eloquently. I immediately began to doubt that I would get the position and no longer wanted to apply.

A law school friend reminded me "if the position is for you, only you can have it." I applied and to my surprise, I was accepted. I was confused on "why" I got accepted when others that I knew were more "qualified" than me did not.

When I arrived in Texas and met my boss for the next 6 months, I knew God had to send me. Prior to going to Texas, I only aimed for goals that were in reasonable reach. The more time I spent with my boss the more she encouraged me to reach for the impossible. Her entire life's journey she reached for the impossible.

From that point on, I was still afraid when I pursued other opportunities but I never doubted what God could do for me if I trusted the process.

# PHASE 6:

## ACCOUNTABILITY PARTNERS

*"As iron sharpens iron, so one person
sharpens another."*

What are accountability partners? These are the people that are sold out on your vision. There is no convincing them. They see the vision and they get it and they won't compromise even when you want to give up. They are the people that you can confide in and will know when to nurture you and when to slap you back into reality.

They are the people that won't take "no" for an answer and refuse to allow you to produce mediocre work because you feel that it's "too difficult." Please choose these people wisely. You must trust them with your vision. There will be individuals that will only serve as an accountability partner for one major step in the process.

Trust is key here because there will be moments they have to tell you things you don't want to hear. However, you have to be assured that they have your best interest at heart. Their intentions and motives are pure. They are also aware of their position and your place in the process.

Their goal is to keep you on task and offer wise counsel, not to rearrange or redefine your vision. These individuals won't be angry when you don't take a suggestion or prefer another idea. They know that the vision belongs to you and their primary role is to be a cheerleader, counselor, aid, and whatever else may be needed during your difficult times. We should have accountability partners for every goal.

Some of your accountability partners may serve for more than one goal. Choose carefully and wisely. DO NOT, I REPEAT, DO NOT pre-qualify your friends based on your friendship alone to serve as accountability partners. They will support you anyway. If possible, this person is someone that may have conquered this area in their own life, or someone that is on the journey with you to conquer it.

It's easier to follow and submit to authority when you know that person has conquered that area in their own life. If you're constantly questioning advice and second-guessing the knowledge shared, because the person hasn't completed that task, you will stay confused.

For example, if you're trying to buy a house, you're going to talk to other homeowners that have endured the process successfully. We trust people based on their experiences. I have friends from law school that I trust with my life.

Although we are all on a major learning curve I know they have been trained and equipped to find the answer for any problem. I trust them even though they may not have certain experiences, because I know if they don't have the answer they will find someone with experience that does have the answer.

These people can serve as accountability partners, and some of them were accountability partners for this project.

## **TYP Tilling Your Purpose with a Busy Schedule**

I was in a *"situationship"* while in college **situationship:** *not officially dating but passed the ("just friends" stage).*

I always want to execute everything I do with a spirit of excellence, so I try to give my best at all times. To be at the top of my graduating classes required an intense level of focus on my studies to produce the level of excellence I knew I possessed.

I also worked, participated in ministry, assisted other organizations and volunteered. I did all of this before the situationship, so naturally the last thing that was added was the first to be neglected.

Over time, I just couldn't give the time needed to the situation because it wasn't as important to me as my other goals. Well we can't treat God's work that way. We can't say if I have time in my schedule I'll try to do it. We must make time and be intentional about Kingdom Assignments.

Sometimes, we are busy working towards goals in life and God randomly drops something in our spirit for us to do. It may be something as small as giving a friend a phone call to encourage them or starting a prayer line.

We must not take the visions, goals, and dreams that God graciously gives to us and put other things first because our plates are too full to have another assignment. There will be moments when you will have to neglect some things on your schedule, to accomplish what God has assigned to you.

When I studied for the Bar Exam, I kept my phone on "do not disturb" for almost 3 months. Only

5 people had access to me during this time. I missed a lot of moments in my family and friends lives but it was necessary to pass the test.

There will be seasons that you will not be available for extracurricular activities because you are preparing to plant seeds and you need to till the soil. Everyone will not understand. The people that are meant to be in your life will forgive you and move on.

## *Surely I Am My Sister (SIAMS)*

## God's Timing Not Your Timing

In March 2015, I was living in Austin, Texas working an intense externship for the House of Representatives in the 84th Legislative Session. My work days were full morning and night. And yet, God began to download directions for an organization he had given me the prior year.

I was so excited because it was something new and different. I thought that I would be overwhelmed because of the work load, but every time I worked on the organization it wasn't draining but refreshing.

Work began to get more intense as the hours grew longer with each passing week of session. It was toward the end of April that I realized deadlines for my externship were quickly approaching and I wasn't near finishing my assignments.

One of the requirements for the externship was a research paper. I told God that I would have to stop working on the organization project to complete my assignments for my externship.

My externship assignments were not due until July 1. However, I wanted to turn my assignments in a month early, by June 1, before I moved back to Louisiana on June 3. I knew when I returned to Louisiana I was scheduled to start a clerk position the following day and attend summer school that night. I was trying to be proactive and balanced. Well, I didn't consult with God about the plan because it just made sense at the time to put the organization on hold.

May 1, I ceased all work toward the organization project and directed all of my attention to completing my assignments. The entire month of May, I may have written a few of the 25 pages that were due.

I felt like I wasted a month of my life. I didn't get anything accomplished for my organization and didn't get any assignments completed for my externship. When I returned home and worked for the clerk position, the work inspired me to write the research paper for my previous externship.

When summer school and the clerk position ended, I told God I was ready to start working on the organization again because I had more time. Well, he never said anything. After taking a moment to evaluate the year, I realized months later, that God's timing was perfect.

If I would have moved according to God's timing the assignments for the organization could have been finalized while I was in Texas. If I remained obedient concerning the organization in Texas, at the time that God was speaking about it, I could have taken advantage of the opportunity to partner with another organization in August for a huge kingdom assignment. God knew that I had the assignments for my externship due. He also knew when I returned to Louisiana my new clerk position would have sparked something in me to write the research effortlessly.

He also knew that when I returned to Louisiana my schedule would be consumed with school, ministry, work, family, and so many other distractions. His timing is always perfect and we have to be careful not to miss it. I missed it.

God was trying to birth something through me while I was away from the distractions of life, but I missed it. I was so hurt and disappointed in myself because I didn't get it right and I missed the opportunity to work with God.

I prayed, repented, and moved on because I couldn't afford to stay stuck. God was still waking me up every day so I knew future assignments would come and I needed to be in a posture to hear from Him the next time another opportunity presented itself.

I knew the season for that particular assignment had passed but I told God I would try my best to get the future opportunities right.

We have to be careful not to allow the hurt and pain and disappointment from our mistakes to influence how we proceed in the next season and with the next assignment.

God began to speak about the organization again this year. Immediately, I began to make provisions, in spite of the other projects going on, because this time I won't miss the importance of his timing.

# PHASE 7:

## PURE HANDS AND A CLEAN HEART

There are a few questions that you should ask yourself before proceeding. This part is purposely not placed in phase 2 because you needed time to settle your mind. Now that our minds are settled, and we have our fight songs, and we are ready to create, there are a few questions we must ask ourselves.

What is motivating you? What are your intentions?

If you are unsure, these questions may help:

**A. Do you know if the goals listed are your desires or God's desires?**

**B. Why do you want to accomplish this goal?**

**C. What purpose will this serve in your life?**

**D. Who will benefit? You? Others? Both? How?**

**E. Your timing or God's timing?**

These five questions will help to position us in life. It reminds us of what is important, who is important, and most of all, why we are choosing to be uncomfortable and choosing to be stretched. It explains why we are willing to inconvenience our lives. These questions provide substance to your foundation. They remove the shallowness from the bark of the tree we're trying to grow. They reassure us that come rain, snow, storm, it is still worth it.

If you are motivated to do something because others are doing it or to prove others wrong or to outshine others, let me offer you a different perspective on life. If you are fueled by "haters" and negative energy, you can accomplish your goal outwardly but will suffer from inner turmoil, bad feelings, unforgiveness, and many other issues. The best way to keep your head and heart clear is to stay in your lane and complete your work to please God.

Don't compare yourself to others and stay away from people who are not supportive. Birthing and creating something new is a very vulnerable place. The people you surround yourself with can build you or tear you down.

When I decided to start SIAMS (Surely I Am My Sister) I wanted to help young women like me. I wanted to offer intelligent young women guidance at the most critical point of life. I wanted to encourage and reassure them that they would be great in spite of any obstacles that they may have faced.

My success in law school was solely to show by example that we are fearless and wonderfully made women who can do all things through Christ. My career, business endeavors, personal relationship with Christ are all fueled by knowing that there are young women that will desire to do something great and will be faced with obstacles beyond their control, but if I can share my resources, my story, and knowledge with her, not only will she accomplish her goals but she will reach back and help others do the same!

The vision has to outlive you. The legacy must continue when you're gone. Don't do it for social media or your haters. Do it for the countless others that have died for you to have the opportunity. ***Pay homage to the lives lost by being a lifeline to the next generation.***

Now that you have refined your "why," let's get creative.

## <u>TYP Tilling Your Purpose in Rejection</u>

I wanted to start a project and I knew some people in the field but when I presented the idea to them they didn't agree with my method. Shortly after, I received feedback from others that were not able to assist with the project. Well, God gave me the assignment so I knew it was purposeful and I knew it had to be done by a certain time.

After the feedback, I assumed that maybe I missed a step. I was unsure and stopped working on the assignment. Months passed, and God presented the opportunity to follow through with the project through a different person, and I did. Later God revealed to me that I went to familiar territory because it made sense to me. We have to follow through with the vision but also be led by God to partner with the right people to execute it.

There will be moments when everyone will not agree, understand or see the vision, Build Anyway! The rejection is not to hurt your feelings it's used to get you comfortable with everyone not agreeing with you and to protect you from traps that seek to destroy what God is trying to build.

The project had to be fulfilled at that particular time because up until that point, I never followed through with my personal assignments from God. It was easier to help others build their visions, dreams, and goals, instead of working on what God had given me. Although I was assisting with major Kingdom assignments for others, I was still disobedient because I allowed my time to be absorbed and didn't complete the kingdom assignments God had given me.

It was more than another assignment for the Kingdom. God was testing me. He wanted to know if He could trust me. He wanted to know if I would be easily moved by the opinions of others. He wanted to see if I was willing to stand in opposition. If I couldn't handle other's opinions or rejection at this level, I wasn't prepared to go to the next level.

God will test you to see if He can trust you! Can God trust you with the vision?

# PHASE 8:

## REWARDS

*"You Will Reap What You Sow"*

Rewards are gestures that celebrate an achievement on your journey. Rewards should be granted when you arrive at a milestone on your journey. The reward should be realistic and measurable according to the level of achievement. Don't forget to record the date of the milestone and the type of reward given.

When we work on projects and meet our goals, we immediately want a reward. When we plant seeds in certain areas, we expect a return from where we planted the seed. Nothing worth fighting for is obtained without a fight.

More often than not, we will plant a seed in one area and reap a harvest from a different vineyard. As we uplift, encourage, share resources and create opportunities for others, someone somewhere will be led to do the same for us and our children.

We are all currently partaking of the fruit from the seeds that our ancestors planted. They knew when they planted certain ideas, shared visions and dreams, and strategies, that they would never get to see the fullness of the legacy. They planted the seed anyway because they knew if they planted good seeds we would one day need them. The harvest of legacy is rich not in monetary things but in character and morals and values.

What you put out is what you should expect to get back. If someone has been working on their business for 10 years, they will most likely meet goals that someone who has started 3 years ago will not meet. It's a matter of patience and persistence. Don't allow someone else's path to deter you from your own.

Social Media portrays images of everyone "living their best life." Prior to "living their best life" there were many tireless nights, early mornings, tears, disappointments, and discouraging moments that made them want to throw in the towel.

The fruit that you see is from there consistency and unwavering commitment to the vision in spite of. "You will reap if you faint not," means we should anticipate that the obstacles we have to overcome are going to be intimidating. However, if we endure with His strength all things will be possible.

"To whom much is given, much is required" means that the greater the reward the greater the responsibility. The rewards are always available to us. The benefits of pursuing our dreams and goals are available to us, but it all comes with a price.

The difference between the person you are today and the person you aspire to become will be determined by the cost you are willing to pay to get there. You reap what you sow. If you sow positivity, love, joy, wisdom, commitment, discipline, and peace it will come back to you.

## **TYP Tilling Your Purpose Through Insecurities**

My thoughts: Everyone is writing a book. Everyone has a nonprofit. Everyone has a business. Everyone is doing the same thing.

God's Perspective: No one is doing the same thing because no one has the same experiences. We may all sit in the same room at the same event but our experiences will all be different because we will process it from different perspectives.

It's the same in business. There are many people offering similar services, but no one can offer an experience like you without you. You don't have to worry about the business growing and people liking it because those whom you were created to reach, will identify with your experience. No one can ever take your experience away.

There will be other stories filled with more theatrics, sad moments, triumphant moments, but if the people can't relate to the experience, it will just be a story.

In order to separate yourself from just another moment, choose to be vulnerable and share life changing purposeful experiences. Count on the fact that, regardless of what other stories are like, your story is a story that has never been told.

In a world full of stories, someone is still waiting to hear your experience so they can say and feel that out of the billions of stories around the world in your story, "I hear me, I feel me, and I see me."

It's imperative that you address your insecurities early on before they turn into jealousy and envy toward your brother or sister. Always check your perspective and heart while tilling your purpose.

Don't allow your insecurities to keep you from making a divine connection, a fruitful friendship, or life-changing mentoring moment. Insecurities will have you critical of others and their work and producing nothing of your own. Everyone has to pay a price for their success. Spend more time learning and taking notes, and less time criticizing.

## *T-Shirts*

I was working on a huge faith based conference and graduating from law school the spring semester of 2016. It was my last semester of law school and I was taking more classes than suggested, which was a norm for me.

However, this semester was a different test of faith. Usually when I work on a God sized goal, toward the very end of the goal being accomplished there is crazy opposition. This time was <u>beyond</u> crazy.

I knew that my faith would be tested from working on the conference, because the devil is always upset when kingdom work is going forth. I knew that my faith would be tested from my last semester of law school because the same thing happened in my last semester of undergrad and graduate school.

One day, I was working on the budget for the conference and I was getting slightly nervous. We committed to a contract for a God-sized cost and had to wait on God to meet the need.

It is the most uncomfortable position to ever wait in. As the deadline approached God consistently reminded me that He was faithful. The more He reminded me, the more I reminded others around me that He was faithful. After a while, it became my slogan for the semester! And He was indeed faithful.

It was during this trying semester that God gave me the idea to start making shirts and he gave me the writing he wanted on each shirt. Initially, I was excited because I truly believed in it. I began to research everything about shirts from the brands to the various printing processes, etc.

After too much research, I finally sat down and began to work on the idea. Shortly after I got the font, the process of printing I wanted and the colors, I ran into a problem. I gained weight, so I didn't want a fitted shirt, I wanted a shirt that would make me feel comfortable. I spent another 2 weeks researching different styles of shirts. After a while, I couldn't find a shirt that I was totally comfortable with wearing. Long story short, I never printed the shirts.

The shirts weren't my idea. God gave the idea to print the shirts because there were other people that were going through similar life situations that I just went through who needed to have assurance that God was faithful. The purpose was to encourage other people to keep pushing in that real difficult spot.

I missed the purpose of the assignment. I got caught up in my own insecurities, my weight, and my own issues and missed my mission. I missed the moment to partner with God to change other people's lives.

I gained the weight at a very difficult and stressful time and never lost it. The thought of it made me angry and instead of doing something about it, I let it be. Well, because I didn't deal with the insecurity of the weight. I allowed it to make me insecure in carrying out an assignment implemented by God. I took a purposeful kingdom building moment and neglected it because my focus went to fashion and comfort. Don't choose comfortable situations over Kingdom assignments.

Don't let that be you. It's not you. Not anymore.

# PHASE 9:

## VISUALIZE

*Studies show that if we see it, we connect with it, and desire it more. Pictures and videos remain in our brain.*

This phase will allow our creativity to flow. It moves us from paper to poster board. Some ideas on moving in this phase:

i.   Consider drawing your vision board on white printing paper first
ii.  After you've worked through the kinks, draw on poster board.
iii. Powerpoint, Canva, and other digital resources may be used in addition to paper

It may take time to gather pictures, draw, and create elaborate boards. This step should be finished within a week's time. Work on a piece of it every day. As you accomplish your goals, use stars and tabs with dates to mark that the goal was completed.

*Photo Credit: Richie Holmes Grant*

*Photo Credit: Carlie Page, Carliepage.com.au*

## TYP Tilling Your Purpose in Unfamiliar Territory

One day I had to minister for a conference, but I didn't know anyone that would be attending. I knew a few people that helped plan the conference but I didn't know anyone personally. I began to feel nervous and alone.

**My thoughts:** *"I'm not going to do well. I just need to see one familiar face that will make me feel comfortable."*

God reassured me that He was enlarging my territory, and in order to enlarge my territory He had to put me in rooms with people I didn't know. If I stay working with people that know my name and are familiar with me, my territory couldn't be enlarged. What appeared to be a lack of support was orchestrated by God to stretch, expand, enlarge, and increase.

## *Lack of Knowledge is Not Lack of Support*

When we embark on new adventures we hope to have the love and support from our loved ones. Unfortunately, when we don't get the reaction we hoped for, we assume that those individuals don't support us.

I believe that a lack of knowledge can be confused with a lack of support. I have friends who were also first generation college students. They were trailblazers for their families. After undergrad, some of us decided to go to graduate school.

One of my friends enrolled in graduate school when she found out she was pregnant. Initially, she thought it was impossible to work full time and go to graduate school while pregnant. She discussed her plans with some mutual friends and we all told her to enroll anyway.

We knew there were many people in graduate schools that were married and had a family. She was encouraged but when she had a conversation with her family and other friends they disapproved.

Their responses were hurtful and she really took it to heart. I talked to her again and she decided to enroll anyway. She did very well her first semester. The baby was due the following semester and she anticipated sitting out and returning in the summer.

When she received her grades from her first semester she was excited and proceeded to enroll in the spring and take all online classes so she wouldn't miss anything when she had the baby. Her GPA was still above a 3.0 after the spring semester.

She graduated on time, with us, from graduate school and her baby, husband, friends and loved ones were there to witness and cheer her on. Initially, she felt unsupported and was upset with her loved ones, but she didn't understand what was happening at the time.

I explained to her midway through her master's degree how we have to be sensitive to those around us that don't have access to the information and experiences that we take for granted sometimes. Her family and friends were always supportive of her and they wanted the best for her. The advice given to her in the beginning of her journey was based on their life experiences.

They assumed that school would be too much stress on her and the baby and they wanted her to have a healthy pregnancy. They feared the worst, and their concerns were valid—based on their life experiences.

Whenever you discuss college with a group of people there will always be pros and cons depending on who is sitting in the room. If you sit in a room with people that didn't go to college or have never seen it in a positive light, there may be some resistance. If you sit in a room with doctors, lawyers, engineers, and scientists, college will be the only option.

We have to sit in the room with people that are currently where we want to go. We can't take it personal or get offended when others don't understand, because we will miss the opportunity to change their minds.

My friend is about to graduate with her Ph.D in the spring. Several women in her family have attended or went back to college because they saw her persevere and graduate.

She didn't allow her frustration to block her from being touchable to her family that are now encouraged to walk in her shoes. It's not always a lack of support, sometimes it is a lack of knowledge and experience.

# PHASE 10:

## COMMITMENTS

*"Commit! Commit! Commit!"*

The difference between who you are and what you accomplish today, and who you will be 3 years from now will be determined by what you are committed to today. Vision takes time to manifest and it manifest in phases.

The seeds you plant today may not feed you tomorrow but will feed your children later in life. You will never know and your children will never know who you are until you commit to your purpose and fulfill it daily.

## Commitment:

*Will you take this vision to be a part of the necessary steps to fulfill the purpose God has for you? Will you love and obey the vision giver?*

*Will you stay committed through good and bad to His vision assigned to you?*

*When you get sick and tired or when you can't see or feel Him moving, will you stay Faithful to the vision?*

*Will you pour out God's plan until you are completely empty and God refills you for the next vision?*

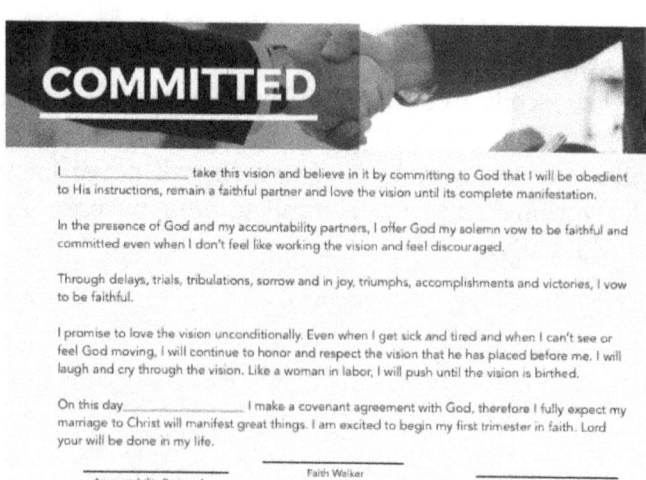

**COMMITTED**

I_____ take this vision and believe in it by committing to God that I will be obedient to His instructions, remain a faithful partner and love the vision until its complete manifestation.

In the presence of God and my accountability partners, I offer God my solemn vow to be faithful and committed even when I don't feel like working the vision and feel discouraged.

Through delays, trials, tribulations, sorrow and in joy, triumphs, accomplishments and victories, I vow to be faithful.

I promise to love the vision unconditionally. Even when I get sick and tired and when I can't see or feel God moving, I will continue to honor and respect the vision that he has placed before me. I will laugh and cry through the vision. Like a woman in labor, I will push until the vision is birthed.

On this day_____ I make a covenant agreement with God, therefore I fully expect my marriage to Christ will manifest great things. I am excited to begin my first trimester in faith. Lord your will be done in my life.

_____      Faith Walker      _____
Accountability Partner 1                                       Accountability Partner 2

# The MANDATE

A **pink slip** is a notice of dismissal from employment. The definition for "employ" is, *to give someone work and pay or compensate them for it.* **Work** is defined as *an activity of mental or physical effort to achieve a purpose or result.* There has been a mandate on our lives since conception to steal, kill, and destroy us and everything we do. The employment rate for the enemy is increasing daily because we are allowing them to work in our lives. We give opponents access to our minds and physical bodies. The enemy and his team are making overtime and bonuses on our behalf. It's time we hand out a few pink slips. It's time for us to stop answering the door and inviting the enemy in to discourage us and keep us from pursuing our purpose. It's time that we meet him with pink slips. It's time for us to stop hosting interviews with negative people, depression, insecurity, doubt, fear and poverty and sharing our vision moving forward. The enemy will change form and pretend to be on your side to get hired. He will interview successfully for the job. We have to stop employing him. When negative people, depression, insecurity, doubt, fear and poverty come, we must stand and say there is no work for you in our houses/ temples, in our dreams, goals, and visions. We must stand in authority and fulfill the purpose God intended for us to complete.

Every assignment to deter or delay or destroy the vision is cancelled. There will be no more procrastination, no more slothfulness, no more feeling defeated, no more feeling discouraged, no more feeling unqualified. This time we will start and finish our goals and leave the strategy for the next generation to do the same. Our visions, ideas, dreams, and goals will leave a generational legacy of blessings and heavenly bounty.

# Acknowledgements

My desire to share AIM HIGH was driven by my village. "It still takes a village" and I am indebted to all of my loved ones for extending that love to me. It was through your love and support that I endured, overcame, and conquered areas in my life that propelled me into my purpose.

The strongest woman and most forgiving person I know, my mama, April Marie, is truly one of a kind and there aren't enough words in the world to express my gratitude and appreciation for her support emotionally, spiritually, and financially. There were moments when she didn't see or understand, and yet she still believed and supported me. I know God immensely loves me because He chose me to be your daughter. I thank you for teaching me how to be confident, resilient, and always a lady.

I'm truly grateful for my father and Pastor, Preston Jones, for stepping out on faith, trusting God and allowing me to express my gifts. I thank you for reminding me to be anything I want to be.

My grandmothers, Marie and Vermell, bestowed unconditional love, guidance, and rearing, without them, I wouldn't be here today.

I would like to thank my mentor, midwife, and spiritual grandmother Carmen Bazile, thank you for fighting for me during times when I couldn't fight and teaching me how to fight for myself. To my great grandmothers Marguerite and Marilyn, thank you for always being on my side.

My aunts, Rhonda and Marilyn (Nook), were always my biggest cheerleaders, the countless sacrifices they made to see me have a better life, and sharing their life experiences to guide me is priceless. Thank you both for being unique in your own special way, I love you dearly.

It was my amazing siblings that made me pursue what appeared to be impossible. I am forever indebted to them and am extremely proud of each of them, Mikella, Michael Jr., Preston Jr., and Joshua.

Nylah, Aliyah and Allison, it's a privilege to influence your lives, I will always love you for being you.

My Godparents, Yolanda, Darnell, and Katrell, were there to fill in the gaps, thank you for supporting my parents through covering me.

My large families: Womack, Jones, Thomas, Griffin, Hawkins, and Alexander, thank you for loving me, covering me, and protecting me.

I have the best sister friends on this side of heaven, I love you dearly, you are simply the best. I'm grateful for the covenant between us and your love extended to me in my valleys and your support on the mountain. I look forward to growing grey hair with each of you.

My City of Refuge Family, allowed me to learn, grow, and evolve. Thank you for your prayers and support.

My Sister Love Family, thank you for your unwavering support, love and reminders of who I am in the Kingdom.

I want to thank Pastor Julia Myles, it was sitting before you that God first spoke to me about writing a book. I'm glad I didn't give up on the vision because you were also the connection to ensure the vision came to pass. Thank you for leading by example.

To the amazing powerhouses that broke glass ceilings and taught me to AIM HIGH because "only your best will do" S. Mandisa Moore, Professor C. Reed, Professor M. Burden, Dr. Margaret Burnham, and Rep. Senfronia Thompson, thank you for revealing the truth and seeing the best in me.

"If the ax keeps hitting the tree, the tree will eventually fall" thank you Professor Vance for directing my swing because the tree indeed fell.

My research mentors, Dr. Willie Kirkland and Dr. Leslie Grover, encouraged me to AIM HIGH and only accepted my best work. They taught me to work through the pain, and prepare for the gain. I am forever indebted to them for demanding greater of me.

For reminding me that my mistakes made me beautiful and to always write the "real" story, thank you Kalamu Ya Salaam and Jim Randels and the entire SAC family.

To Mama Liberty, Broderick, and my FYS family, thank you for giving me the mic and exposing me to a global mindset. I know I'm worthy of speaking because of your teaching.

For keeping me accountable to the vision, thank you to my publishers, The Legacy Project and your entire team for your quality work and effort.

A huge appreciation to Ashley, for allowing me to see her journey behind the scenes, "it takes all of that and a whole lot more." I'm eternally grateful to you because it prepared me for this moment.

Lillian and Crystal counseled, advised and provided an honest perspective on this project, and I'm indebted to each of you for laboring in prayer and expertise on this project.

Neisha, thank you for being a listening ear and speaking life to my purpose, this project would not have been completed without your commitment to the vision.

To my mentees and little sisters, thank you for being silent accountability partners to all of my goals. Your presence is truly a lifeline for me, every time I wanted to give up, I thought of you and got back up again.

Last, and most important, I am grateful for the countless people that have trusted me with their visions, dreams, goals, mistakes, downfalls, pitfalls, and life's most tragic and heartbreaking moments, your testimonies encouraged me to AIM HIGH in spite of life's circumstances.

Thank you.

*THE END!*